KIP KEINO

by
Wayne Coffey

BLACKBIRCH PRESS, INC.
Woodbridge, Connecticut

Published by Blackbirch Press, Inc.
One Bradley Road
Woodbridge, CT 06525

©1992 Blackbirch Press, Inc.
First Edition

Manufactured in the United States of America

10 9 8 7 6 5 4 3 2 1

Editor: Bruce Glassman
Photo Research: Grace How
Illustrations: Richard Smolinski

Library of Congress Cataloging-in-Publication Data

Coffey, Wayne R.
    Kip Keino / Wayne Coffey. — 1st ed.
    (Olympic Gold)
    Includes bibliographical references and index.
    Summary: Describes the athletic accomplishments
of the Kenyan track star who won gold medals in both
the 1968 and 1972 Olympics.
    ISBN 1-56711-003-7
    1.Keino, Kip, 1940-   —Juvenile Literature.
2. Runners (Sports)—Kenya—Biography—Juvenile
literature. [1. Keino, Kip, 1940-   . 2. Track and field
athletes 3. Blacks—Kenya—Biography.] I. Title.
II. Series.
GV1061.15.K4C54 1992
796.42 '092—dc20
[B]   92-16253
                                                 CIP
                                                 AC

96w3004

Contents

1

Just a Kid from a Village

"I run because I enjoy running."

ne day when Kip Keino was a young boy, he was out walking in the mountain air near his family's home. The Keinos lived in the East African country of Kenya. Their home was a mud cottage in a small farming village with a very large name: Kapchemoiymo. The village is located near the Equator.

Opposite:
Kip grew up in East Africa, where life was sometimes difficult and dangerous. He learned early about the advantages of running fast and far.

Hiking over the rugged terrain, the youngster looked up and suddenly froze. His eyes widened in fear. Kip was face-to-face with a hungry leopard, which was preying on a goat that had been grazing on the nearby hillside.

Kip backed away slowly, being careful not to make any sound that might startle the animal. When he felt it was safe, Kip broke into a sprint. His heart pounded through his thin chest as he raced past rocks and jumped over brush. He ran and ran until he was pretty sure there wasn't a leopard on his tail. Kip just kept steaming along at the same swift pace. He didn't get tired.

We will never know how fast or how far Kip Keino ran that day. We don't want to know what would have happened if the leopard had chased after him.

What we do know, however, is that the scared young boy would grow up to be one of the greatest Olympic distance-runners in history. And he would do it with a simple approach. As Kip once said before a race, "I just figure to run as hard as I can, as fast as I can, for as long as I can. I run because I enjoy running."

A Personal Approach

Most expert runners are very scientific in their approach to running. No detail is overlooked. They regularly consult with their coach about such things as the length of their stride, their breathing, and their running techniques. They keep a stopwatch handy, carefully recording their times over different distances. They want to know how fast they cover the first half-mile, or the last half-mile, so they can fine tune their training in the area where they need it most. With such precision, the run-

As Kip once said before a race, "I just figure to run as hard as I can, as fast as I can, for as long as I can."

ners believe they can shave a few precious seconds off their time—these seconds can often mean the difference between winning and losing a race.

Kip Keino followed none of the practices of other expert runners. Especially in the early part of his career, his approach was simply to lace up his track shoes, report to the starting line, and take off. He thought nothing of running 5,000-meter and 10,000-meter races in the same day—which also went against accepted track practices.

Without a community of expert runners around him, Kip developed a method that worked for him. He ran long and hard every day, building up endurance and speed. He didn't know about state-of-the-art running and training techniques. But he knew that he wanted to finish first. And very often he did just that.

A Meet in London

Seasoned track-and-field observers were astounded by Kip Keino's results. Several years before he became an Olympic sensation, Kip participated in a meet in London.

7

Running in the one-mile race, he won in three minutes, 54 and two-tenths seconds. His timing was just six-tenths of a second off the world record at the time. And the mile was not even his specialty! Kip liked to run it just to improve his overall running speed, since the pace is faster than the pace of the longer races. After his victory in London, Kip said he was so focused on his running that he lost track of how far he had run. He wasn't even sure when he had entered the final lap.

"I had no idea I would do this," Kip later said, smiling.

Few of the spectators at White City Stadium could believe what they had just witnessed. As one sportswriter said, "Now let me get this straight. This Kip Keino comes straight out of the mountains of Kenya, and runs a mile just because it's good for his speed. He doesn't know anything about his lap times, and then he comes within a whisker of breaking the world record. I have just one question then: How fast is this man going to go once he knows what he's doing?"

After his victory in London, Kip said he was so focused on his running that he lost track of how far he had run. He wasn't even sure when he had entered the final lap.

The answer: very, very fast. And it wasn't long in coming.

2

Hero for a Nation
"The George Washington of African runners."

ip Keino's first race came when he was a 13-year-old schoolboy. Running against kids who were bigger and faster, Kip finished fourth, an impressive showing given the competition. Afterward, he was awarded his first prize—a bar of soap.

The youngest of six children, Kip Keino was born into a family of the Nandi tribe in January 1940. His full name was Kipchoge (KIP-choke-ee), though most people knew him by its shorter form.

The Nandi tribe is found in western Kenya, a rural area where people live in poverty. Medical care in the region was

extremely scarce when Kip was growing up. Four of Kip's brothers and sisters died as infants. His mother died when he was just four years old.

Kip's father had a small farm where he raised goats. Because there was no public school system in Kenya, Kip spent most of his time on the farm, too, herding goats with his father.

The youngster wanted to attend a school in the village. He would often ask his father if he could enroll. It was very hard for his father, because he needed help around the farm and because the school was more than he could afford. But Mr. Keino could see how much it meant to his boy. Kip enrolled in school at age 12, and stayed for four years.

It was while he was at the school in Kapchemoiymo that Kip won the soap. He did not take running too seriously then. It was not as if he had visions of becoming a world-famous athlete. He just loved running. It was a fun thing to do.

A Young Police Officer

Kip set many running records at the school. He didn't really think about competitive running until he joined the Kenyan police academy at age 19. The academy was located in the town of Kiganjo, near Mount

Placing fourth in his first race at school earned Kip Keino a bar of soap.

Kenya. It is a mountainous region, with peaks of 6,000 feet. In the lush, tropical mountains, Kip Keino, the young police officer, first began to realize the extent of his talent.

The academy had a variety of sports for the officers to participate in. Kip quickly established himself as one of the best athletes ever to come through the police school. One quality that stood out most was his excellent conditioning. At 5 feet, 9 inches and 145 pounds, he was strong and lean. It is much more difficult to run at high altitudes, because there is less oxygen in the air than there is at sea level. This didn't bother Kip Keino, who ran as if he had his own private oxygen tank strapped to his back.

Kip quickly established himself as one of the best athletes ever to come through the police school. One quality that stood out most was his excellent conditioning.

After he had been at the academy for several years, he was made a physical-training instructor. He helped his fellow officers improve their own fitness, and was able to devote more and more time to running.

Right around this time, in 1963, Kenya won its independence from Great Britain. Kenya had been a British colony for nearly 75 years. Just as when the United States celebrates its independence on July 4 each year, the estimated 10 million people of

Kenya felt a tremendous sense of pride in their new national identity. Kenyans started to seek out heroes for their infant nation. Kipchoge Keino's fast feet quickly made him one of the country's leading candidates.

A Role Model for the Young

The British had introduced a variety of sports and competitions into Kenya during their rule. But until it gained independence, sports had never been much a part of Kenyan life. The new Kenyan government expanded the school system, and physical education became more important. Young Kenyan children had greater opportunities to join in sports and games. Before Kip's Olympic career was over, it was common for youngsters to dash around school-yards and declare, "I want to be just like Kip Keino."

Somebody once tagged Kip as "the George Washington of African running." Indeed, many other African countries were gaining their independence around the same time as Kenya. These nations also started sports teams. All over the continent, people were proud that an African native, Kip Keino, had sped to the forefront of running in the entire world.

Word of Kip's impressive efforts spread rapidly. Not long after he started running

13

competitively, he set Kenyan records over one, two, and three miles. In one busy day at a police championship meet, he smashed the existing records in three events: the one-mile, the two-mile, and the six-mile. Was he tired? Not so tired that he didn't run in a 440-yard relay.

In 1962, Kip traveled to Australia to participate in the British Commonwealth Games. He ran in the mile and the three-mile, and held the lead in both events after bolting to his typically fast start. The other runners, far more experienced, paced themselves well and Kip fell back into the middle of the pack. But even though he didn't win, the trip provided Kip with

valuable experience. It was his first major international competition. It gave him a sense of the pressure involved, the attention, as well as the tactics of a number of the world's most seasoned runners.

Then Kip qualified for the Kenyan Olympic team for the 1964 Games, which were to be held in Tokyo. Few people outside Kenya had heard of Kip Keino by then. Kip chose to compete in the 1,500-meter and 5,000-meter runs.

In major meets such as the Olympics, competitors must qualify in order to get to the finals. To qualify, a runner has to be among the top finishers in preliminary races known as *"heats."*

The 1962 British Commonwealth Games were Kip's first major international competition. Although he didn't win, he learned what it takes to become an Olympic athlete.

15

In the first heat for the 1,500, Kip was the top finisher. Then, in the semifinal heat to determine the finalists, he ran almost four seconds faster—clocking a mile in three minutes, 58 and nine-tenths seconds. It was a promising showing, but not quite good enough. The race featured some of the best milers in the world. Kip's time did not quite qualify him for the Olympic final.

However, the 5,000-meter run was a different story. One of Kip's opponents was an Australian named Ron Clarke, who would set the world record a year later. Running in a heat against Clarke and others, Kip Keino stuck right with Clark and finished just a second behind him. Kip had qualified for the finals, but it was the way in which he did it that grabbed people's attention. He seemed to run so effortlessly, with his graceful, loping strides gobbling up the ground.

Chance for a Medal

Kip was thrilled. His dream was to win a medal for Kenya, and now that he was in his first Olympic final, he had a chance to do just that.

The 5,000-meter final was a closely contested race. The finish line resembled a rush-hour train. There were five men within a second and a half of one another. As they strained toward the finish-line tape, each man dug in, trying to forget the fatigue and pain. The winner, in a major upset, was Bob Schul of the United States. Schul shot ahead of all the favorites over the final 300 meters.

In fifth place, but not very far behind Schul at all, was Kipchoge Keino of Kenya. Kip was disappointed not to have secured a medal, which he missed by a fraction of a second. But when he looked at the larger picture, he had to be pleased. He was competing in the first Olympics of his life, and he was only 24 years old. As far as running went, he was just a baby, certainly compared with his Olympic rivals.

In the 1964 Tokyo Games, Kip proved to the world that he was a worthy contender for an Olympic medal. His fifth place finish in the 5,000-meter final was only several seconds behind the winner, Bob Schul of the United States.

17

When any athlete competes on the world stage for the first time, it's only natural to have doubts about whether he will be able to measure up. This is particularly true for athletes from small or developing countries.

At the young age of 24, Kip made an impressive showing at the 1964 Games in Tokyo.

Kip Keino entered the Olympics with many questions about how he would do. Now, his questions were answered. Even though he finished fifth, he realized that he wasn't out of his league by any means. He was one of the best 5,000-meter runners in the world.

Kip headed home with growing self-confidence. He was inspired by what had happened in Tokyo. Kip Keino knew greatness was within his reach. "Now I'm going to go get it," he told himself.

3

An Overnight Sensation

*"When I feel confident I will win,
I take off the cap and throw it."*

K ip returned to the academy in
Kiganjo after the Tokyo Olympics.
He resumed running on the steep
slopes in the shadow of towering
Mount Kenya, which rises 17,040
feet above sea level. He continued
to serve as an instructor, teaching the finer
points of volleyball, gymnastics, and bas-
ketball. But he devoted most of his energies
to running. He was already the world's
fastest policeman. The joke was that you
didn't want to be a criminal if Kip Keino
was walking the beat, because there was
no chance of outrunning him.

After drawing some attention in Tokyo,
Kip burst like a comet on the world track

scene in 1965. Almost overnight, he became the sport's greatest sensation. Track fans on every continent were talking about his smooth-flowing stride, his lively manner—and his hat.

When Kip was in Tokyo, he purchased an orange baseball-style cap in a souvenir shop. Later, he started wearing it during races to shield his eyes from the bright lights overhead. He developed the habit of tossing the hat from his head when he sensed victory was his.

"It's like a signal to the crowd," Kip said. "When I feel confident I will win, I take off the cap and throw it."

Kip loved running and competition. The huge crowds he attracted sensed his enthusiasm. His smiling, easy-going nature was as much his trademark as his speedy pace.

In London, in the summer of 1965, Kip won the mile in a time of three minutes, 54 and two-tenths seconds. He became the first African to run under four minutes. Kip would go on to run the mile under four minutes more than 30 more times before he was finished.

Track fans on every continent were talking about his smooth-flowing stride, his lively manner—and his hat.

But his mile feat was nothing compared to what he did in Helsinki, Finland. Competing in the 3,000-meter run—a distance of about two miles—Kip won the race

Kip's baseball cap became his trademark for winning. A toss of the cap in the air showed the crowd that he felt he would be victorious.

easily. But what everyone was buzzing about was his record time of seven minutes, 39 and four-tenths seconds. Kip Keino had set a world record. Nobody in track-and-field history had ever covered 3,000 meters so swiftly.

A Broken Record in New Zealand

Later in the year, he was on the road once more, this time to Auckland, New Zealand. He was entered in the 5,000-meter run. Six months earlier, Australia's Ron Clarke— one of Kip's Olympic rivals in Tokyo—had set a world mark of his own in this event. Clarke barely had time to get his trophy up on the mantel, because his Kenyan foe broke the record at the New Zealand meet. Kip's clocking of 13 minutes, 24 and two-tenths seconds surpassed Clarke's mark by just over a second.

Ron Clarke had a chance to regain his record in December 1965, however. He and Kip competed head-to-head on Clarke's native turf, in the city of Melbourne, Australia. The noisy crowd was pulling hard for its national hero to win, and maybe even to break the record again.

Clarke was regarded as among the hardest working runners in the world. He ran an average of 150 miles every week, almost an unheard of total. Kip Keino, on the other hand, had an entirely different philosophy. On a typical week, Kip would run under 40 miles. However, Kip was doing that running in the thin air of the Kenyan mountains, which made the workouts far more strenuous than they would be at a lower altitude. That made it a little easier for him to run at lower altitudes. Kip also mixed in a great deal of speed work, running at full throttle over shorter distances, such as one-quarter mile. His belief was that the mixture would give him the endurance to last over a long race, and the pure speed to outrace his opponents when he needed to.

In the Melbourne race, Ron Clarke moved out to a small lead when Kip was briefly boxed in by a couple of runners. Kip quickly realized he was in danger of letting Clarke get away. He squirmed free from the crowd and quickly joined Clarke at the head of the pack.

The two runners stayed together as they matched each other stride for stride around the grass track. The pace wasn't going to break Kip's record, but the drama built steadily. When they turned into the final lap, Kip made his move, boldly and confidently. He surged a few strides ahead. He kept sprinting and headed into a turn,

Kip Keino had set a world record. Nobody in track-and-field history ever covered 3,000 meters so swiftly.

23

Kip and Australian runner Ron Clarke had a showdown race in Melbourne, 1965. The close race became a major upset in the final seconds, as Kip pulled ahead to win by almost 40 yards.

building a bigger and bigger lead. Kip felt strong. He felt he could maintain this blinding pace and leave Clarke in his dust.

The Australian tried to go with him. He desperately pushed himself to go faster. But he just couldn't do it. Kip was far ahead by now, running like a hare. Ronald Clarke felt a bit like a turtle.

Kip Keino's remarkable last lap produced a victory by almost 40 yards. A close race had become an upset in a matter of seconds. The crowd was stunned. Clarke was, too. It was clear that Kip's incredible speed work had paid off.

"Every time I surged forward, I could hear Keino puffing behind me," Clarke said afterward. "I thought this indicated he was tiring. But then he kicked past me so fast I knew I couldn't match him in the sprint home. I had to be content to watch him draw farther and farther away from me."

First-Time Runs in America

Every year in the United States there is a series of indoor track meets in the winter. Kip Keino, the sport's brightest new star, was the major attraction at those meets in the winter of 1965-66. Running in the United States for the first time, Kip was nipped at the end of the mile in the Los Angeles Invitational, finishing second. His disappointment did not last long. Ninety minutes later he bounced back on the wooden track for the two-mile race. Kip breezed to victory, and had a chance to toss his orange hat toward the end.

His next stop was New York City, where he won the mile at the Millrose Games, perhaps the most glamorous indoor meet of all. Kip Keino had established himself as one of the most awesome middle-distance

runners anywhere. Photographs and articles featuring Kenya's most famous policeman now appeared regularly in newspapers from Boston to Brussels. He continued to rack up triumphs. Before long, it was time for another Olympics.

During the winter of 1965–66, Kip took the United States athletic world by storm.

The year was 1968. The place was Mexico City. Kip turned his focus toward his most cherished goal: earning a medal for Kenya.

4

Getting the Gold

*"I want to run every race I can,
for I owe it to the people of Kenya."*

A s the 1968 Olympics approached, a
great deal of the attention in track
and field had shifted away from
Kipchoge Keino. The most her-
alded runner was a young, dark-
haired American named Jim Ryun,
from Wichita, Kansas. Jim Ryun had a long,
loping stride, and was being hailed as one
of the great finishers in running history. In
track, they call the sprint toward the finish
line the *"kick."* Even when he was still a
teenager, Jim Ryun's kick was feared by his
rivals around the world.

Jim arrived in Mexico City as the world
record holder at 880 yards, 1,500 meters,

and the mile. He was considered a big favorite to capture the gold medal in the 1,500. His record time of three minutes, 33 and one-tenth seconds was nearly four seconds faster than Kip Keino had ever run. Four seconds may not seem like much, but in a race of that length it is a sizable chunk of time.

Olympic Face-Off

Jim Ryun and Kip Keino had competed several times, and the American had won every time. In fact, Jim defeated Kip in the race in which Jim set his record. Still, most experts felt that if Jim was going to be beaten in the Olympics, Kip would be the one to do it. The Kenyan did have one noteworthy advantage. The altitude of Mexico City was 7,300 feet. Kip had spent his whole career running in high elevation. He was as accustomed to thin air as any runner in the world. Jim Ryun's native Kansas, on the other hand, is low in elevation and flatter than a pancake.

Kip didn't just have Jim Ryun to worry about, by any means. In fact, the swift Kenyan may have been the busiest man in all of Mexico. Besides entering the 1,500, Kip chose to compete in the 5,000 and 10,000-meter runs, too. When you include the runs to determine who would make the finals, this meant he had to run six grueling races in eight days. And each time out, he would be up against the best runners in the entire world.

Few athletes would even consider such a triple event, believing that running all three would make it impossible to perform their best in any of them. But Kip Keino had supreme confidence in his conditioning. At 28 years old, he was in his prime. He had never worried before about the accepted wisdom of the sport. He wasn't going to start now.

Health Troubles Begin

The one concern Kip did have, though, was his stomach. He had been suffering from sharp pains for some time. The pains would get almost unbearable at certain moments, and other times would lessen. It wasn't until the Games were over that Kip discovered that the problem was a serious gallbladder infection.

His doctors had cautioned Kip about the problem before the Olympics began. It's important to give your body plenty of rest, they had told him. They strongly suggested that he not run in all three races. But Kip was firm about his plans. The Olympics come along only every four years, he told himself. "I will have plenty of time to

recover afterward," he thought. "I want to run every race I can, for I owe it to the people of Kenya, and to myself."

The schedule called for the 10,000-meter run to come first. As the demanding race unfolded, Kip Keino was running with the leaders, along with fellow Kenyan, Naftali Temu. As the laps passed and the drama built, several runners fell way off the pace. The runners passed the 8,000-meter mark. Kip continued to run with strength and confidence. The 10,000-meter distance race was hardly Kip's specialty, but you would never have known that from his pace.

As the leaders raced on, Kip crumpled to the infield, doubled over with cramps, caused by what would later be diagnosed as the gall-bladder problem.

And then, suddenly, Kip felt a sharp jab of pain in his stomach. The pain quickly worsened. Kip could barely stand. As the leaders raced on, Kip crumpled to the infield, doubled over with cramps, caused by what would later be diagnosed as the gall-bladder problem. A medical team raced toward him with a stretcher. When Kip spotted them, he scrambled to his feet. It was hard to tell whether the worst of the pain had passed, or if his pride refused to let him be carted off from an Olympic event on a stretcher. Kip bravely got back on the track. He couldn't run fast, but he was determined to finish what he had started.

During the 10,000-meter event in the 1968 Olympics, Kip doubled over with severe stomach pains. Pushing himself to the limit, he managed to get back up and finish the race.

It was a bitter ending for Kip Keino. Th only consolation was that his fellow Kenya Naftali Temu, spurted past Mamo Wolde Ethiopia in the last 50 meters. Temu wc the 10,000 by two strid capturing the first track-an field gold medal of the 19(Olympics. Kip was thrill for his teammate, but he al had to live with disappointment. He h; wanted badly to be the first Kenyan to w a medal.

Kip was thrilled for his team-mate, but he also had to live with disappointment. He had wanted badly to be the first Kenyan to win a medal.

Four days later, the two Kenya returned to the track for the 5,000 mete It was a tight race fiercely contested l three Africans: Kip, Temu, and Moham Gammoudi, a 29-year-old soldier from T nisia, a country in north Africa. Gammou was a bony, 135-pounder. How he ma aged to weigh so little was puzzling. A cording to one account, Gammoudi had fi cups of yogurt, ten pieces of fruit, four cu of tea, two cups of coffee, two pastries, a plenty of meat, fish, milk, and cheese every day! It's a wonder he could get out bed, let alone streak around a track.

And streak Gammoudi did. He was clir ing to a narrow lead with just two laps to ; Kip made a charge at him. Naftali Ter also challenged to take over the lead. Ea time one of his rivals tried to motor by hi

(Continued on page

1968
MEXICO CITY, MEXICO

KIP BURSTS ONTO THE SCENE

Right: 1965 was a banner year for the young runner from Kenya, Kip Keino. In Auckland, New Zealand, Kip broke the record for the 5,000-meter race previously set by Australian Ron Clarke. Kip's time of 13 minutes, 24 and two-tenths seconds was more than a second faster than the standing record.

Above: Kip and Ron Clarke run neck-and-neck during a 5,000-meter contest in Stockholm, Sweden, in July 1965.
Right: Running in his trademark baseball cap, Kip takes the lead in the Los Angeles Invitational Track Meet two-mile run in January 1965. Kip won the race by a wide margin.

Taking America by Storm

After winning races in Los Angeles, Kip went on to New York to compete in the Millrose Games, one of the most glamorous events in track-and-field competition. At the Millrose Games, Kip won the mile race and firmly established himself as one of the world's leading middle-distance runners.

Below: Kip's publicity shot, taken just before the Millrose Games.
Right: Back in Los Angeles in 1967, Kip became friendly with U.S. super-star rival, Jim Ryun. At the 1967 United States-British Commonwealth track-and-field meet, Kip and Jim competed against each other in the 1500-meter and the metric-mile events.

THE GAMES IN MEXICO CITY

Above: The Olympic flame burns after being ignited by Mexican athlete Enriqueta Basilio, the first woman to light the flame.
Right: In a closely contested 5,000-meter race, Kip narrowly lost the gold to Mohamed Gammoudi (left) of Tunisia. Kip (far right) took home the silver medal for placing second. Also shown are Naftali Temu (center) and Ron Clarke (right).

Kip embraces Naftali Temu after Temu won the gold medal for the 10,000-meter competition. The race was a bitter disappointment for Kip, who crumpled over in pain during the event. Kip's only consolation was that Temu, a fellow Kenyan, won the race and Kenya's first track-and-field gold medal in the 1968 Games.

THE 1,500-METER SEMIFINALS

The most dramatic competition for Kip in the 1968 Olympics was the 1,500-meter race. Jim Ryun was heavily favored to win the event having won the 1,500 by wide margins in previous competitions. Here, Ryun breaks the tape in the semifinals with Kip close behind.

KIP'S INCREDIBLE VICTORY

In the final 1,500-meter event, Kip knew he was up against the toughest possible competition. When the race began, Kip got off to a blazing start, followed closely by fellow Kenyan Ben Jipcho. With 200 meters left in the race, Jim Ryun tried to burst forward to overtake Kip in the lead. Even though Ryun narrowed Kip's lead, he could not catch up in time. Kip won the race by more than 20 meters—the widest margin of victory for that event in Olympic history. Kip's time of three minutes, 34 and nine-tenths seconds was also an Olympic record.

Above: After winning the 1,500-meter gold, Kip trots around the track in a victory lap with teammate Ben Jipcho.

Right: The awards ceremony for the 1,500-meter race. Kip (middle) stands with his gold, while silver medalist Jim Ryun (left) shakes hands with bronze medalist Bodo Tümmler of Germany.

KENYA'S OLYMPIC HERO

Upon returning home to Kenya, Kip and his teammates were honored by Kenya's president Jomo Kenyatta at an official ceremony in Nairobi. Here, Kip presents the president with a small replica of his Mexican gold medal.

1972
MUNICH, GERMANY

MISFORTUNE OPENS A DOOR

Above: The qualifying heat for the 1,500 finals in 1972 was a devastating disappointment for Jim Ryun, who fell and sprained an ankle in the race. Kip, who won the heat, consoled Ryun after the race.
Right: The finals for the 1,500 was a close contest between Kip and Pekka Vasala of Finland (center). As they streaked toward the finish side-by-side, Vasala burst forward to take the gold from Kip, who settled for the second silver medal of his Olympic career.

A Sweet Swan Song

The 3,000-meter steeplechase was the final event in Kip's Olympic career. Although he had little experience in the event, he went on to win the gold by setting an incredible Olympic record of eight minutes, 23 and six-tenths seconds. After his victory, the crowd in Munich rose to its feet and cheered one of the greatest runners of all time.

(Continued from page 32)

Gammoudi successfully fought off the threat. The race came right down to the wire, with Gammoudi trying to hold on, and Kip Keino hot on his heels. Over the final 100 meters, Kip did all he could to overtake Gammoudi, but the Tunisian was just a little too strong on this day. Gammoudi held on to win, in a time of 14 minutes, 5 seconds. Kip Keino earned the silver medal. Only two-tenths of a second separated him from the gold. Naftali Temu, meanwhile, picked up his second medal of the competition, taking the bronze.

An Eye on the Gold

Although it was a fine accomplishment for Kip Keino to finish second, it only heightened the importance of the 1,500-meter run. Kip wanted to go home with a gold medal. He knew that this wasn't his strongest event. And of course he knew he had to contend with the remarkable Jim Ryun, who had not lost a race at this distance in more than three years.

The day didn't start in a promising way for Kip. Leaving the Olympic village in the congested streets of Mexico City, he got caught in a traffic jam. Cars and buses were snarled up as far as he could see. The longer he sat in the mess, the more anxious he became.

Race time was approaching. It was crucial that Kip have plenty of time to warm up and get totally focused for the race. He decided he couldn't afford to wait in the tangle of traffic any longer. He hopped out of the vehicle and ran the last mile to Olympic Stadium.

A Blazing Start

As he thought about the upcoming race, Kip knew he needed a strategy that would protect him from Jim Ryun's famous kick. In race after race, Ryun had stormed from back in the pack to take the lead in the final 300 meters or so. Kip always preferred jumping out to a fast start.

"I feel that when you're in front, you control the race," he said once. "Those people who run behind cannot run fast."

His plan wasn't merely to get a good start. He wanted a blazing start. The high altitude wouldn't hinder him, as it might other runners. There was no reason to be cautious. Kip decided his best shot at victory was going all out, and hoped he could hold on when Ryun kicked into high gear.

Over the first 400 meters, yet another Kenyan, Ben Jipcho, led the pack. Jipcho raced to one of the fastest starts in Olympic history, covering those first 400 meters in just 56 seconds.

Kip Keino was flying. His time for 800 meters was one minute, 55 and three-tenths seconds. Most of the fans were certain he would pay for this in the end.

"No way he can keep this up," many people said.

Kip had left the pack—Jim Ryun included—in the distance. He steamed into the third lap with a huge lead. Jim Ryun was stunned by what Kip was doing. He was also a little nervous. It's a very hollow feeling for a runner when he sees a competitor as great as Kip Keino surge that far ahead. If a less talented runner did it, Jim Ryun wouldn't give it a thought. He would know that the runner would start to slow, and probably wind up behind almost everybody else.

Still, Jim was determined not to panic. He didn't want to kick too early, because then he would have nothing left. Why change strategy just because this lightning bolt from the Kenyan mountains was

Kip had left the pack—Jim Ryun included—in the distance. He steamed into the third lap with a huge lead.

treating the race as if it were a dash? Jim figured the best course was to wait for Kip Keino to run out of gas. Then Jim would make his move.

Jim Ryun's tactics were perfectly sound. The only trouble was that Kip Keino was hardly slowing down at all. It was near the

end of the third lap, and the Kenyan's lead was still enormous. Jim Ryun couldn't afford to be logical anymore. He had to go and get Kip Keino.

Ryun bolted away from the other runners and went after Kip, who knew this was coming sooner or later. Jim Ryun's long, fluid strides glided over the track. The gap was closing. The fans were in an uproar now, enthralled at the drama that was unfolding before them.

Kip was fading a little. He pushed himself as hard as he could as he turned into the final 400 meters.

Kip was fading a little. He pushed himself as hard as he could as he turned into the final 400 meters. He knew the closer Ryun got, the more confidence and encouragement the American would have.

"Here's the famous Ryun kick," Kip thought. "I've just got to keep going and fight him off."

With about 200 meters left, Jim Ryun narrowed Kip's lead to about 12 yards. Kip didn't want to look over his shoulder. He pushed himself with all he had to maintain his speed. Jim Ryun was running bravely, showing tremendous courage. It looked as if the Kansas native was going to make it a race to the finish, after all.

The two running legends stretched out their stride, each giving it absolutely everything now that the finish line was in sight.

Jim's kick seemed to be fading a bit. The gap wasn't narrowing anymore. As they entered the home stretch, it was clear Kip Keino was going to hold him off. Jim Ryun had expended so much energy making his final charge that he had nothing left for the very end.

Kip crossed the finish line more than 20 meters ahead of Jim Ryun. It was the widest margin of victory in the 1,500-meter run in the history of the Olympics. Kip's time—three minutes, 34 and nine-tenths seconds—was also an Olympic record. It was almost two seconds better than he had ever

Kip breaks the tape for an Olympic record in the 1,500-meter run during the 1968 Games. Fifteen yards back, in second place, is Jim Ryun of the United States.

run before. It was the second fastest time in world history. The only man ever to run faster was Jim Ryun.

For Kip Keino, it was the thrill of a lifetime. He trotted around the track arm in arm with Ben Jipcho. The crowd saluted him with a deafening roar. His Kenyan teammates mobbed him. A tremendous sense of elation washed over him. All the years of sweat and training had paid off. Kip Keino was an Olympic gold medalist.

A tremendous feeling of elation washed over him. All the years of sweat and training had paid off. Kip Keino was an Olympic gold medalist.

He smiled and celebrated for a long time. And believe it or not, that day—October 20, 1968—got even better a little later. Back in Kenya, Kip's wife gave birth to their third child. It was a girl. They named their new little girl Milka Olympia Chelagat. Her middle name was a special way for Milka's father to always remember his precious moment, thousands of miles from home, in the thin air of Mexico City.

5

A New Challenge
"I had a lot of fun..."

Ten days after his historic Olympic triumph, Kip Keino and his fellow Kenyan heroes were honored in a victory parade in the capital city of Nairobi. It was a festive occasion in the young nation, as people poured into the streets to celebrate the team's great accomplishments. It was very moving for the athletes to get this sort of reception.

The parade was making its way through the city streets when suddenly Kip slumped over. A hush fell over the crowd. Kip was rushed to a hospital. It turned out that he had fainted and was suffering from more painful complications of his gall-bladder infection. Kip underwent an operation to

remedy the problem. No doubt the doctors were totally correct when they told him not to subject his body to too much stress.

Kip gradually regained his strength, and before long he was back in his old form. He continued to be one of the leading performers in international running.

Another Shot at Glory

In 1972, at age 32, Kip elected to take a shot at more Olympic glory. This time, because of a scheduling conflict, Kip entered only the 1,500-meter run and the steeplechase, a demanding event in which runners must not only cover 3,000 meters, but also clear 7 water jumps and 28 hurdles. The steeplechase is perhaps the most unusual running event of all. Fans see quite a spectacle as the competitors vault the hurdles and splash through water, then quickly settle back into their regular stride.

Before the finals of the 1,500, Kip had to run in a qualifying heat. One of his rivals in that race was a very familiar face: Jim Ryun of Wichita, Kansas. Usually, the leading runners are placed in separate heats, to give them the best possible chance to meet in the final. But that didn't happen this time because of a computer error.

Jim Ryun is one of the great American distance runners in history. But he had the misfortune to suffer his worst moments—and worst luck—in the Olympics, when the whole world was watching. With just over 500 meters to go, Jim started to move toward the lead when he got tangled up with another runner. He lost his balance and went crashing to

The winner of the heat, Kip Keino, went over to his long-time rival. Kip had great respect for Jim Ryun's ability. Kip put his arm around Jim and tried to console him.

the track. Appearing dazed, he lay on the track for eight seconds before getting back on his feet and making a desperate spring to catch up to the pack.

But he had lost too much ground. It was hopeless. Ryun suffered a bruised hip, sprained ankle, and a concussion in the fall. Later, he said, "All I know is everything was going well, and I felt good. And the next thing I knew I was trying to figure out what happened."

Jim Ryun was devastated. Tears filled his eyes when the race was over. The winner of the heat, Kip Keino, went over to his long-time rival. Kip had great respect for Jim Ryun's ability. Kip put his arm around Jim and tried to console him. He whispered some kind words of support. It was a compassionate gesture. But the fact was that right then and there, nothing was going to lift the hurt that Jim Ryun felt.

In the 1,500-meter final, looking to defend his Olympic title, Kip made a surge

about halfway through the race. He broke from the pack, and his chief rival, Pekka Vasala of Finland, broke with him. They raced together the rest of the way, Kip trying to bolt away from him, and Pekka Vasala sticking to him like mud on a shoe. As they streaked toward the finish after the final turn, Kip still held a narrow lead. Then, the Finnish runner, knowing this was his last chance, spurted by Kip, into the lead. Kip tried all he could to find the energy for another surge of his own, but he just couldn't do it. Pekka Vasala edged him to win the gold. Kip Keino settled for the second Olympic silver of his career.

A New Challenge

Kip then turned his focus to the steeple-chase. This was an event he had rarely competed in. By no means was Kip experienced at dealing with the water and the hurdles. He entered the race because he wanted a new challenge. He was convinced he had the necessary agility and fitness to make a good showing.

The 3,000-meter steeplechase would turn out to be the final Olympic event of Kipchoge Keino's eventful career. And he went out in a blaze of glory, because Kip didn't just capture the gold medal. He did so in an Olympic record time of eight minutes, 23 and six-tenth seconds, just one second ahead of his Kenyan colleague, Ben Jipcho. Jipcho appeared to have a great shot at winning at the end, but Kip—taking a page from his friend Jim Ryun's book—outkicked Ben to earn the victory.

Huge cheers filled Olympic Stadium in Munich, as the crowd honored one of the greatest runners of all time. In the track world, coaches and athletes were amazed at Kip's feat—winning the gold in an event he was new at. But it only seemed to be Kip Keino's way of doing things.

At the Munich Games in 1972, Kip ended his Olympic career with a dramatic win in the 3,000-meter steeple-chase. He completed the event in a record time of eight minutes, 23 and six-tenth seconds, to win the gold.

Running was always something that was pure and full of enjoyment for Kip Keino. The steeplechase was no different. He laughed about his bad form clearing the jumps. He said he looked like an animal going over them.

The steeplechase was just another instance of Kip Keino marching to his own beat. He trained hard, as he had for so many other events. He believed in his own ability. He didn't get overly concerned with what the so-called experts were saying, about whether they thought he had any chance at all to win. What mattered most was what Kip Keino himself thought he could accomplish and what he enjoyed doing. "I had a lot of fun jumping the hurdles," he later commented.

Kip competed a few times after the Munich Olympics. Here, he easily beats longtime rival Jim Ryun in a mile event in Los Angeles, 1973.

After all, Kip Keino spent years just coaching himself. He had no stopwatch, no specific practice routine, and little technical command of the sport's finer points. He would just head into the mountains and run. He would listen to his body. He learned exactly what he could do and couldn't do. Over the years, he became as much of an expert in the art of running as anyone. Although usually it's the observer who sees best, in Kip's case, it was the runner himself.

Passing the Torch to a New Generation

Now Kip Keino is passing along that knowledge. He has a group of running pupils in Kenya. One of them is a young man named Martin Keino, who is Kip's son. Martin has developed into an accomplished runner in his own right. Early in 1990, at age 17, Martin ran a mile in four minutes, 17 and eight-tenths seconds at a track meet in Los Angeles, California.

"He's doing much better at his age than I did," Kip said. That means Martin Keino probably has quite a future on the track ahead of him. We already know he has quite a teacher.

Glossary

altitude The measure of height from the earth's surface or from sea level.

diagnosed Looked at and classified by a doctor.

equator An imaginary circle around the earth that divides the earth's surface into two equal parts, north and south; regions near the equator are usually hot and dry.

fatigued Tired or exhausted.

gall bladder A pear-shaped sac that stores bile in the body.

heats Preliminary qualifying races.

kick The sprint towards the finish line.

meet A sporting event in track; a competition.

meter Basic unit of length in the metric system, equals 39.37 inches, or 3.28 feet.

opponent A competitor.

pace The rate of speed in walking or running.

relay A team race, each member runs separately in turn.

rival One who competes against another.

steeplechase A race in which runners must clear hurdles and water jumps along the course.

Further Reading

Aaseng, Nathan. *Track's Magnificent Milers.* Minneapolis, Minnesota: Lerner, 1984.

Arnold, Caroline. *The Olympic Summer Games.* New York: Franklin Watts, 1991.

Arnold, Caroline. *The Olympic Winter Games.* New York: Franklin Watts, 1991.

Bailey, Donna. *Track and Field.* Austin: Raintree Steck-Vaughn, 1991.

Tatlow, Peter. *The Olympics.* New York: Franklin Watts, 1988.

Index

A
Auckland, New Zealand, 22, 34
Australia, 14, 16, 22

B
Basilio, Enriqueta, 38
British Commonwealth Games,
14

C
Clarke, Ron, 16, 22–25, 34–35,
38

E
Ethiopia, 32

F
Finland, 20, 46

G
Gammoudi, Mohamed, 32, 38,
49
Germany, 42

J
Jipcho, Ben, 42, 50, 54, 59

K
Kapchemoiymo, 5, 10
Keino, Kip
final Olympic event, 48,
58–59
first Olympic gold medal,
53–54

first race, 9
health problems, 29–30,
55–56
1972 Olympic Games, 45–48,
56–59
1968 Olympic Games, 15–17
1964 Olympic Games, 30–44,
49–54
at the police academy, 10
as a physical training instructor, 12, 19
running in U.S., 25, 35, 36
schooling, 10
tossing his hat, 20, 25
training routine, 7, 23, 61
Keino, Martin (son), 61
Keino, Milka Olympia Chelagat
(daughter), 54
Kenya, 5, 9
independence from Great
Britain, 12–13
Kenyatta, Jomo, 44
Kiganjo, 10, 19

L
London, 7–8, 20
Los Angeles Invitational, 25, 35

M
Melbourne, Australia, 22–23
Mexico City, 26, 27–28, 33,
38–43 49, 54,
Millrose Games, 25, 36
Mount Kenya, 10, 12, 19
Munich, 45–48, 58–59